The Impressionist

Shailesh Patil

BookLeaf
Publishing

India | USA | UK

Presentation by *BookLeaf Publishing*

Web: www.bookleafpub.com

E-mail: info@bookleafpub.com

ISBN: 9789360945022

First edition 2024

"To the Creator, whose infinite wisdom has granted me the gift of experiencing life in all its myriad forms; to my beloved parents, whose unwavering love and guidance have been my constant companions as we navigated life's unfolding journey together; to my esteemed Gurus, whose patient wisdom and guidance have sought to quench my insatiable curiosity and illuminate the path before me; and to myself, for embracing the challenges and joys of self-discovery, and for having the courage to embark on this poetic odyssey."

ACKNOWLEDGEMENT

To my father and my mother who fostered in me the love for language, and my teachers who gave me an opportunity to express in various forums.

PREFACE

Within the realm of art, the term "impressionist" carries a rich history, embodying a style that emerged in the late 19th century. Impressionist painters, with their loose brushwork and emphasis on capturing fleeting light and atmosphere, sought to convey the essence of a scene rather than its precise details. Yet, the essence of "impressionism" extends far beyond the canvas; it permeates the very fabric of human expression.

Just as painters evoke moods with strokes of colour, so too can writers and musicians paint with words and melodies. In literature, an impressionist approach invites readers to delve into the subjective experiences and perceptions of characters, rather than dwelling on objective facts. Similarly, in music, impressionist composers weave intricate harmonies and textures to evoke mood and atmosphere, transcending the boundaries of mere melody.

In this collection of poems, I invite you to embrace the spirit of impressionism in its broadest sense. Each verse is a brushstroke, capturing fleeting impressions and emotions with the delicate precision of an artist's hand.

Through these words, I endeavour to convey the intangible essence of life itself – its joys, sorrows, and everything in between.

As you embark on this poetic journey, may you find solace in the transient beauty of each moment, and may these impressions linger in your heart long after the final page is turned.

INDEX

She	1
The Flower	3
The Lamp	5
The Priest	7
Childhood	9
The Guiding Light: Ode To My Mentor	11
Worship	12
Salutations To A Tinkling Dime	13
The Idol	15
Churning Of The Ocean	17
The Raw Materials	19
The Incense Stick	21
My Desires	23
Veil Of Tears	25
My Heart, Her Love	27
The Window	28
In Search Of...	30
The Labourer	32
Birthdays	34
The Paradoxical Age: The Teens	36
The Final Embrace	39

SHE

Narrative: This is an ode to all mothers. She will
remain the first love of my life.

Her treasure of love shared will increase
and degrade it will, on storage,

When this secret was revealed
and the Constitution held out,
I was unaware of a goddess watching me
as I tread on this verdant and bountiful earth.

She remained resolute and steadfast as I
progressed
to maturity and patience,
and susceptible to her I was.

The celebrations and the birthday
when I reached to recognize her,
did reveal some suffering and strife.
I wonder if it was felt
for her face mirrored a glorious miscellaneous
life.

I got a companion and a roof,
all were makeshift structures.
It did reveal the permanency of her hand
as the ultimate shelter.

I may try to repay, but there will always be
a penny less in things offered,
for there will forever exist—-
the incomparable love of mother
with her unchallenged immortality
and price uncounted as my part integral
like a heartbeat—soft, tender, and conspicuous.

The Flower

Narrative: This poem is an ode to the humble flower and an Impressionist way of looking at a flower.

Its tear laments
a sorry departure.
Rapturous smile applauds
a success,
Embracing every protected feeling,
it synchronises itself to the tune of life.

Be he a disgraced sinner
or a leander
or the honoured knight,
Its presence gives a calm relief over isolated
graves.

It was born. The soothsayer said,
solicitous for emotional beauty,
and the world accused it of stealing the thunder!

Yet the subtle ways
of a roseate evening,
gets me overwhelmed with festive Joy
as I touch the manifestation of emotions—the
flower!

THE LAMP

Narrative: This Poem is a take on lost
opportunities, our ignorance, and a dilemma
about life and death—is it continuous or is it
some end or is it some beginning?

The brazen nature around
with glances as beneficence,
why is it blinded to just its sound,
maybe repentance or maybe it's climax!

The incoherent ground and the air smells a
charnel
with effort, I audaciously stare
where life ceases to dwell.

In the tacit night syringe, a systole occurs,
the corpses sink,
as the awesome tableau turns radiant.

An articulate ray of light is incident
on my ignorance—the corpses,
the skipped incentives—the syringe diastole
and the hope I discarded—the LAMP.

The PRIEST

Narrative: The day I was Initiated into the world
of rituals and religious practices, an
impressionist way of looking at the 'Priest.'

Never has he experienced the wound of Life
Still, he has to feel the pain and hear it,
From the truly wretched of the Earth
For whom a lamp of hope has to be lit.

Never has he let a cry a mother
the moment a couple sought the blissful touch of
his feet,
for it's just another parting for him
in whom a tear and a smile meet.

Never has he desired for himself
a share of a darling offering,
through which daft wishes are asked for.
For his sense of duty as the servant of the
Ultimate
abstains him from being an apostate.

A guardian spirit of man he
is not afraid of the missing step
for a thousand hands will stretch
to lead him to the Hall of Deities.

CHILDHOOD

The day before chaos struck
In the prime of my life,
I step out.
Suddenly, the bustling streets seem empty
With no solace,
I stand alone.
A moment before discord arose
Somewhere distant,
Amidst a gathering of loved ones,
A presence fades into obscurity,
With no affection,
I am abandoned.
A glance before I seek an understanding,
In the midst of a bustling city,
A building collapses without warning.
Even nature seems to turn against me
With no reliance,
I am bewildered.

A realization before I lay to rest
My weary body,
Still, my mind remains vigilant.
Noticing my toys – battered and forgotten,
They show no concern, no belief in destiny
I realize I've lost the essence of childhood
Which came too soon, yet too late.

The Guiding Light: Ode to My Mentor

Narrative:
These verses honor the mentors who shape our lives with love and respect, crafted in a sonnet style, encapsulating their role in nurturing our identities.

Amidst the ethereal magic of the sky,
And the serenity of the tranquil virgin nature

All worth more than a sigh
are but signatures of your moral stature.
Surrounded by murky depths of quarrels,
You stand as a solitary herald of peace and morals.
In a disciple's journey, tumultuous and dire,
Amidst haunting competition's fire,
You were the beacon, the lone inspiration,
Guiding us toward the noble's aspiration.
In this ocean of intellects
I consider you as a permanent wave,

Thank you again,

For the invaluable knowledge you gave.

Worship

Alive am I as the blue canopy
where heaven and hell are neighbours.
Demystified and uniform my topography
with friends and foes of any flavour.

An enchanting artefact is this entity
where tempests bow
with music and hymns of purity,
I am an armament of love.

Of heaven and hell the gates may confront,
remain static, or embrace
I will forever flow with no blunt, to give you a
life with grace.

Salutations to a Tinkling Dime

Narrative: The way an Impressionist sees a materialistic world.

Once upon a time, I heard, the tinkling of a dime,
Only to see poverty rush out.
What ensued was a powerful bout.
They say a man is civilised, but
they are just a bunch of snitches
for a dime cannot buy all the riches

Once upon a time, I heard the tinkling of a dime
Only to hear the ensuing sounds of the vendors
for there was a dime among the lenders.
They say the world is a safe place,
But it is just an array of rackets
Safe enough to store the tiny dimes in their
spacious pockets.

Once upon a time, I heard the tinkling of a dime
Only to see the ensuing movement of hands
reach towards their jackets,
for a dime had fallen off from someone's casket.
They say the world is interesting,
But it's merely a façade, a deceptive mimic
no better than a soporific.

Once upon a time, I heard,
the tinkling of a dime.
Only to hear the ensuing words of the people,
"It is a crime for there's always a false time
with whom we cannot dine.
They say this world is full of commotion,
which makes it imperative to say,"
hail a dime, my hearty salutations,
for being the raison d'etre for all the false
notions.

The IDOL

Narrative: This was my Impressionist version of
the idol which we see in all places of worship.

Amidst the everyday walks,
on a small piece of land stood a sanguine
structure.
And that it harboured an Idol
was brought out by the grim looks of its visitors
and its sanctum environs.

Stood it testimony to the changing shape of
candles
and to their fluctuating lights too,
and the idol no longer seemed to respond to its
guests
was shown by many a visitor dropping an
outdated dime.

One day, in a spectacular show of terrible
vengeance,
the Earth parted and sucked into its deep vast
anatomy,
the structure—helplessly non-living,
as the sanctity no longer existed.

Maintaining the sanctum sanctorum
of the small piece of land,
was the Idol—firm and majestic,
in the naked garden.
And it did send the passersby a message...

...that far away deep into their hearts
waiting to wipe a tear and relive an isolation,
is the same 'idol'—enduring and strong,
in a small piece of you, called 'Heart'
and under a broad structure, called 'Mind.'

Churning of the Ocean

This was my Impressionist mind understanding
life post my Yoga and spirituality sessions

The realisation of 'life' as a human,
Is a success of a Malediction.
Do the utmost Good you can,
and render the Hell as fiction.

Embosom the psalms for a journey, perfectly
shaven
And kindle the tempestuous fires.
Destroying the recalcitrant desires,
Is unveiling the way to Heaven.

Mark more fruitful a short-lived existence,
than experience an old age, and bandage the
dead fence.

You are an ocean unto yourself,
Churn it and unearth the hidden treasures,
And enjoy even the short days in full measure.

The RAW MATERIALS

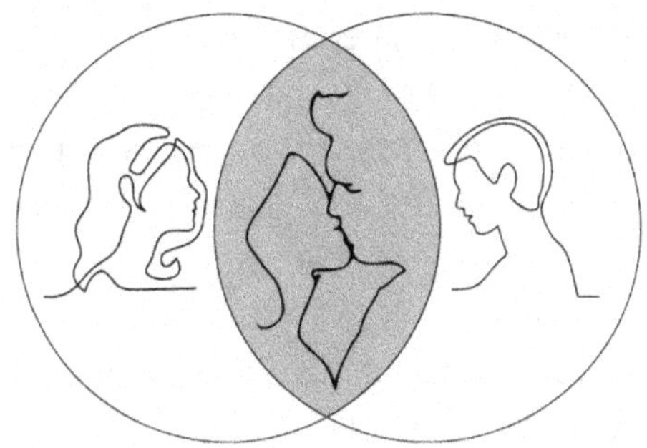

Narrative: This was the culmination of my
Chemistry degree lectures when in college. It is
a funny and humorous take on the subject of
Chemistry and should be taken in good spirits. It
also does not reflect the poet's personal
experiences at all.

In all the catalysts and the indicators of his life's
Periodic table,
she was his AU, AG and Platinum.
They couldn't be inert to any addition-reactions
as their love was destined to glow like a 1000
radium.

Day in and Day out in dreams and thoughts,
Her image occupied the highest density.
Reduction and decomposition never occurred,
as they were inert materials of the highest purity.

Aufbau and Pauli fussed about electron pairing
clever were the ones who discovered electron
sharing.

Of course, the rage among the frigid was nuclear
fission,
the romance was immortal, they underwent
nuclear fusion.

His electro+vity to her electro-vity
Covalent bonds were formed with no resonance,
It was no surprise,
blessed were they with daughter elements!!!

The Incense Stick

In temples grand or humble shrines,
Where sacred whispers intertwine,
There burns a fragrant offering bright,
A dance of smoke in gentle flight.

From a slender stick, a wisp ascends,
A fragrance divine, an aromatic blend,
Of spices, woods, and flowers rare,
That fills the hallowed, tranquil air.

With whispered prayers, it intertwines,
A bridge between the celestials and the earthly,
Each curling plume, a silent plea,
To convey wishes, set them free.

O incense stick, in your slow burn,
Lessons of life, we start to learn,
In your fragrant trail, we find,
A path to peace, a tranquil mind.

From darkness deep to heavens high,
You lift our souls, you help us fly,
In every swirl, a story told,
Of ancient rites and secrets old.

So burn, O Incense stick, burn bright,
Illuminate the darkest night,
With every scent, a memory,
Of love and hope, eternally.

My Desires

Narrative: In today's world, where materialism, consumerism, and instant gratification often dominate, understanding and managing desires can be crucial for inner peace and well-being. However, many times it's too late.

For a living I desired,
I got a life with pas and mas and kins,
Only to find the world—a pile of dreadful sins.

For a company I desired,
I got a friend with vague trends.
With him the journey I continued,
Only to find my desires renewed.

I desired for the happiest wrong,
so, for a partner, I ringed.
Only to find myself, being presented
with an infant-king.

The journey I continued with my offspring,
led me to liars infested with dying desires.

Unaware of the changing strategies,
my future I found myself trapped in difficulties
cause of my excess desiring.

Justice from officials I sought,
and appealed against the debauch.
Only to witness the trial of my desirous
thoughts.

Veil of Tears

Narrative - I have been brought up in times when dowry was at its peak. Every other day, a sister was burnt or harmed in some way. This was despite our rich tradition of keeping the womenfolk on a pedestal. My take here.

Resounding in an atmosphere,
dubiously scandalous,
is the sound of God.
It was in that same spiritual land
that my sister was burnt.

The touch brings forth dodged memoirs.
Oh! the feminine tenderness,
so very much immortal.
It was in this divine moment,
that her hands were reduced to ashes.

One morning the mantra of second life
was to be delivered.
I saw a thirsty hand stretch.
It was in that same liturgical state,
in which a goddess was sold.

Confronted years back, I woke up
to a known cry.
Helplessly shocked, I see a companion.
It was that same mediaeval shriek,
heard from just another bride,
about to be burnt for dowry.

My Heart, Her Love

Narrative: The times when love was in the air.

Amid the romantic gust, I sense
Love's fragrance in the whispering air.
A dream is evolving!
Final touches unveil a marvel,
God's graceful gift- Goddess.

In the heavenly Sunrise, I sense
Golden murmurs amidst the parting beams.
A dream is dissolving.
The enchanting melody of a love bird; brings
forth a companion,
an ideal of Adam- Eve.

In this tender connection, I sense
the flowering of a Bud in romantic realms,
The dream has become a reality.
The dance of excited bees,
brings forth a union,
of My Heart, Her Love.

The Window

Narrative: This is God's / Creator's view of how
he/she must be looking at his/her creation now.

The first glance I cast,
through the consecrated window,
was to appreciate my creation,
a pair of marvellous earthlings.

Armed with a quiver set they
to conquer the subordinates.

Alluring prayers revealed their falsehoods,
for with time, they had multiplied.
Partisan and cannibalism
had settled as their demeanour.

In the grand tapestry of existence,
they lost sight as children of God.
In the allure of power, defeated by ambitions
the true essence was lost.

The false accolades stood testimony,
that was no solution
to an imminent nature's disharmony.
and that was my last glance
through my defiled window,
when I had the weakest arrow
and a profane bow.

In search of...

He bedecks an intelligent physique
A quest in store for him
is realised by the time of twisting fate
Holding a finger for support, he looks yonder
Let himself go off, in search of a golden future.

Beatrice by his hand
He moulids for himself
A monument of identity, to find his place, in
life's eternal embrace.
Feeling lost without a crown heir
He sets forth, in search of a new entity.

The serene toll of bells
Are a countdown to shed blood
for his unending desires.
Ignoring justified obstacles, he advances
In search of a land, where amaranths grow

Breaking archaic shackles
Designed he a model of dreams, yet to appear
still, over the coffins, he is soaring
In search of a land wherein
Horizons Disappear.

The Labourer

In dawn's caress, they awaken, steadfast and
resilient,
Their hands calloused, their spirit vibrant and
gleaming.

Kissed by the sun's first light, a labourer's toil
begins,
They embark on their labour, fulfilling others'
dreams.

Their backs endure burdens,
and brows glisten with sweat,
Yet in their hearts, no space for remorse and
regret.
Sacrificing happiness for their loved ones'
future.

With hammer and nail, they build dreams high,
Amidst the sun's warmth, and under the sky.
From dawn till dusk, their efforts endure,
A testament to strength, steady and sure.

In fields of verdant greens, they work the earth,
Breathing life into seeds, each a new birth.
With weathered hands, they nurture the land,
Harvesters of nature, their purpose grand.

Through heat and cold, through wind and rain,
They persevere, without a complaint.
For in their labour, they find their worth,
Honest and true, from their humble birth.

So let us honour the labourers' efforts
In their toil, in every hour.
From their hands, the world is made,
In their spirit of selflessness, Humanity lives.

Birthdays

Narrative: Birthdays will always come as we advance in age; however, we need to chill and also fully age. More so, in friendship, it's the bond that matters.

This may not happen when the heart is still
It may not happen when the wind doesn't shrill
And this may not happen when life is
non-existent and
Immeasurable distance is persistent.

With illuminated candles on your birthday cake,
Let's laugh at age, for goodness' sake!
Numbers may rise, but our friendship is the
prize.
Cheers to us, for that's where dreams arise!

With each glimmer of flame, your birthday's
embrace,
Let's cherish the years, with laughter and grace!
As numbers ascend, our bond only amplifies,
Here's to our journey, where happiness lies!

In the vast sea of our life to be,
let our birthdays be a wondrous delight to see
that, in the end, when we meet forlorn and
hungry
Let there be a big meal—creamy, munchy, and
free!

The Paradoxical Age: The Teens

From the hands of the divine,
a sacred bestowal,
Into the embrace of Mother Grace,
where blessings flow, is the gospel I carry.

Adorning the mantel of a postulant
I discern new frontiers of knowledge.
Worship and respect to those who fend
Is the duty to which I pledge.

Assuming the psyche of a fetching seeker
I begin to adore the heroes and the sages
To mark a new era with a momentous sculpture
Is the goal that commences on my golden pages.

The incessancy of unsavoury developments
Plunges me into incertitude,
Even in the face of fresh anatomical
amendments
My ideas are put on trial for being a platitude.

Struggling against all odds,
The emerald youth I attain,
Where at the crossroads to God,
I found my prayers on the wane!

A wave of sordid fests
Led me to the penury of hope,
With infatuation in aesthetic pursuits and
Infantilism was what I had to cope!

Climbing the dais on my mettle,
Broke I the traditional vaults
Roared I to be bold and settle
The issue of society and its faults!

From a charming youth to a saint
Experienced I many a 'fears and a smile.'
When the stars in my goal began to faint,
Opened I the desperate file!

Suddenly I heard cries of pain and strife,
I ventured out to find a company
Unaware of the Walpurgis night
A coup I foresaw in my destiny.

Going back through the golden maze
I recalled a miscalculated page
Got I a pinch to my empty doctrines
For inevitably I had an age
Called the paradoxical teens.

The Final Embrace

In this World of a Thousand Millenniums,
bathed in myriad fantasies of
uncontrollable deliriums,
unfolds an eternal voyage of emotional journeys.

A diplomat undertaking a long journey
for a patch-up of medieval feuds,
Evokes memories of a splendid past
Recalling the last agreements.

The odyssey of the Markopolos,
for whimsical escapades it chose,
Instills a hilarious pleasure
Giving me some foolish relief.

An abrupt cry of grief
brings in a downpour of frustrating tears
Only to be consoled by embracing hymns,
The worldly truths of which, discard my
tarnished sins.

In all the kaleidoscopic moods
There emerges an eternal love,
With magnetic instincts – fully decorous to
plow.

As the destination draws near,
A tear falls, bidding farewell to fate's frontier.
Longing for one last embrace, yet resigned,
I humbly withdraw from the illusionary craze,
For, every mortal has to reach his resting place
Into an everlasting embrace.

www.ingramcontent.com/pod-product-compliance
Lightning Source LLC
LaVergne TN
LVHW021305200726
843509LV00012B/1784